THE PUFFERFISH
EFFECT

SUSAN FREW

Frew, Susan, Author

The Pufferfish Effect

Susan Frew

ISBN: 978-1-7336824-0-4

small business and entrepreneurship; marketing

QUANTITY PURCHASES: If you are interested in bulk quantities of this title, contact the author for special terms at https://www.susanrobertsfrew.com/contact/

❀ Created with Vellum

*I dedicate this book to my husband William Frew
for always believing in me before I believed in
myself.*

Acknowledgments

This book would not have been possible without the prayers and blessings of so many people in our community. We started out by praying for work in our small group bible study. So, we humbly apologize to anyone who had a major plumbing issue in Commerce City from 2012-2013, as it was likely the power of our group! I would like to thank our family at Landing Place Church and Orchard Church for calling us first for their plumbing and heating needs. We are grateful for your spiritual cover during times of trouble.

Sunshine does not run without its heart and that's our Sunshine team led by Chris Cannon and Kristie Brown. We have kissed a lot of frogs together and are so grateful we have finally found our royal family!

I would like to acknowledge and recognize my female tribe that would only call Sunshine first, without question: My CampExperience™ Sisters, Colorado Women's Chamber, Women Presidents Organization (WPO), the Women's C3 and the Dames. I love every one of my empowered and brilliant sisters. Thank you, Betsy

Wiersma, Meghann Conter, Cindy Grove and Kristen Blessman for being the influence and "mother" behind these tribes.

When you have had 16 broken bones, 10 concussion and a disease called DISH, your body hurts all.the.time. Without the talent and patience of the ladies at Breath of Life Yoga, I would be immobile. Thank you, Audrey, Nikki, and Tara.

Thanks to Dafna Michaelson Jenet, Michael Jenet, and Christy Belz for the opportunity of the TEDx stage. It was one of the best days of my life.

Thank you, Kris Jordan for so many things written, too many to list!

I am grateful to the business community for their support and more than a few awards since 2012. This includes The Metro North Chamber, Brighton Chamber, Commerce City Chamber, Commerce City Rotary Club, Adams County Economic Development, *The Denver Business Journal*, Colorado Companies to Watch, the BBB of Metro Denver, Congressman Ed Perlmutter, Angie's List, *Colorado Business Magazine*, *PHC News*, Colorado PHCC, PHCC Educational Foundation, PHCC National, and QSC.

Thanks for the friendship and love of so many besties during this process: Debbie and Brad Crowe, Maria Borrego, Kathy Nielsen, Ann and Eric Brown, Lisa and Ken Gochenour, Myriam Parga, Sharon Blackburn, Betsy Wiersma, Kathleen Osgood, Holly Haycraft, Keely Thompson, Blanca Ordaz, Douglas McDaniel and Makenzie Adams McDaniel.

Thank you, Karen Blaney Graves, Jeanine Fattell, Lois Keegan, Dawn Ferrante, Steve Szalus and Bernadine Szalus for being my "life historians" as, after concussion number eight, there are a lot of missing gaps in my memory. I love all of you, and it is a great comfort knowing you are in this world.

Thank you, Aunt Frankie Brown for the story of rag and many others, always unforgettable - I love you.

I am grateful to my daughter Zenaida; sisters-in-law Trina and Rachel; brothers-in-law, Nick and Brian; nieces Katelyn and Patience; nephews Owen, Joey, Nicholas and Matthew for the respite of the Carolina Beach trips. Without this, we would have just kept working and working.

To the marketing and technology genius of Scorpion, Service Titan, and Review Buzz - you make being a Puffer-fish a lot easier to manage. Thank you for the marketing genius of Melodie Reagan and the team at Crazy Good Marketing. Without you, Thriftinista would not exist nor would we be a Pufferfish at all.

Thank you to NSA Colorado and my NSA Master-mind group; Nora Burns, Hilary Blair, John Register, David Dye, Cynthia Staad and Dean Savoca. Although this adventure is just a beginning for me, I am honored and humbled that you invited me to your tribe. Big hugs. Thank you, Traci Brown, for inviting me to NSA- it was a game changer for sure. Life on the road is always better with my partner in presenting, the fabulous Kathy Nielsen.

Our success in business, or mine as a speaker, would not have been possible without the unwavering support of my husband, William. He is my one true love, wind beneath my wings and number one cheerleader at all times. Thank you for believing in me before I could believe in myself. You told me on our first date that I would write a book one day. I love you with all of my heart. Thank you, William for rule #1: Always do Good Work- you are the boiler genius, hands down.

None of Sunshine's success could have been possible

without a very big GOD and His unwavering supply to our company during our growth. There have been so many miracles that have occurred during these years that there are too many to list. All that we are, and all that we accomplish are for His Glory and goodness.

Thank you all!
Susan

Introduction

The truth is I'm blessed. I'm married to the love of my life, William. I'm a stepmom to a great kid and a joyous mom to our rescue fur babies. We also "adopted" our Brazilian exchange student who now lives with us and attends college in the US. I'm a former International General Manager with AT&T Wireless and Business Coach with ActionCOACH. I've been an instructor for the Small Business Administration's Emerging Leaders Initiative and the radio host of "Coaching: Not Just for Sports" on ESPN radio in Denver.

I've coached 150 businesses in 17 trades, helping them to succeed. I've also served as the President of the Plumbing-Heating-Cooling Contractors Association of Colorado and as a Board Member on both the Metro North Chamber of Commerce in Denver and the Adams County Workforce Center. I'm a Trustee for Quality Service Contractors and an Advisory Board Member for the Emily Griffith Technical College.

And I've grown my family's plumbing, heating and air conditioning business from $177,000 in annual revenue in 2012 to over $3 million in 2018.

I have also overcome substantial personal adversity. To date, I have sustained 10 concussions and 16 broken bones. This collection of mishaps comes from a variety of sports, car accidents and an old domestic violence situation. My first head injury was in a car accident circa 1978 when Traumatic Brain Injury (TBI) was not discussed or treated appropriately.

Life sailed along just fine with me crashing while ski racing, mountain biking, etc. In 2010, I had a minor car accident, just touching my head to the steering wheel, which resulted in a week-long blackout. Then four years later, I was accidentally hit by a tether ball and was out of work for close to four months. My memories of life are fuzzy at best; I have lost entire pockets of time in my past. Living life with TBI is not easy, but it is doable when you have an amazing Faith in God and a support system, as I do with my husband and my Sunshine work family.

There are days when I must rest or spend the next three with an excruciating migraine. I know my limits and protect my boundaries accordingly. I share this story not to boast but to encourage. If you live with an ongoing health challenge, do not let this stop you, instead learn to manage around it. I cannot live without my laptop, yoga, Pilates, yellow pads and my notes of life. For the many things I don't remember about my past, I count on my "life historians." They have walked with me for my entire life and can fill in some of the gaps.

But this book isn't JUST about my family business or overcoming adversity. It is about a Jersey girl who fell in love with a brilliant man who is a master plumber and an expert in heating and solar thermal technology. This story is about how, together, we created a business focused on outstanding customer service. We leveraged what was important to our customers to penetrate a saturated market and look bigger than we were, thereby crushing our competition. I call this concept *The Pufferfish Effect*.

Here are some key things to know about pufferfish:

1. They are small but blow themselves up to several times their size when needed.
2. They are among the most poisonous vertebrates in the world. Because of this, they don't hide from predators, but predators who try to eat them will regret it.

While the keys I will be presenting in this book are the exact successes and failures we experienced in our plumbing, heating and air conditioning business, the concepts are transferable to other fields as well. I will explain how they worked specifically in our industry, but I will also provide information that can easily be implemented in any service company.

When I met William, he was running his plumbing and solar company in Breckenridge, Colorado. If you aren't familiar with the area, it's a ski town. Thermal heating is very trendy there to keep ice from forming, to warm flooring, and to heat hot tubs among other things.

After our marriage in 2012, we made a decision to

move to the Denver area, and we were very aware that we had 950 competitors in our market. We knew we wouldn't be able to compete on price, so we had to find a new way. We wanted to create a new standard to present our company in a meaningful way that would leave a mark and grow our customer base.

William and I had both experienced loss from a recent recession. We understood that we needed a business based on service work, because it was recession-proof. New construction failed and big, luxurious purchases fell by the wayside (which is why we wanted to leave the pricey Breckenridge area). People were looking for ways to save money and to keep things working longer – bottom line, service never goes away. Marketing was the key to our plan from the very beginning.

My desire for the readers of this book is that you will discover that marketing can be fun. So many business owners I meet hate the marketing part of business. They try the same things they've always done, looking for different results and getting discouraged. I want you to realize that if you understand and embrace marketing, it doesn't have to be hard. Instead, you can make it fun and have a good time with it. Think of it as a game instead of a drag.

I hope this story inspires you to do things differently. I hope this book equips you with solid how-to steps to implement in your business that will render your competitors unimportant. I hope you learn how to use a great reputation to look bigger, better and more desirable to your customers. I hope you become the business you yearn for. I hope this helps you to become a Pufferfish.

How to Be a Pufferfish

WHEN I DECIDED TO WRITE THIS BOOK, I REALLY WANTED it to be a how-to guide to help business owners do what we had done to make our company successful. This means I had to look closely at what we did and break it down into easy, doable steps. I also knew it had to be something any business could do regardless of your marketing budget or how long you've been in business. In addition, I needed to point out where we made mistakes along the way, so you could learn from our experiences. Some of the things we implemented worked while others flopped. The important thing is that we always knew what we wanted to accomplish, so we just kept trying different ways to make it work toward that end.

I want you to do the same thing as you look at these steps. First, get clear about what your end game looks like and then implement and adjust, or as Dory from *Finding Nemo* would say, "Just keep swimming." We are pretty sure she's friends with a pufferfish, so we take her very seriously. Business isn't about setting something in place and forgetting it. When people do this, their company ends up closed, or they are sitting in coaching sessions with me saying, "That's the way we've always done it."

It doesn't matter to them if what they have always done isn't working anymore. Frankly, they may not even know if it is working or not because they've taken their finger off the pulse and stopped tracking it.

We NEVER say, "It's the way we've always done it" as justification for why we do anything. We are quick to make changes when we see a better way, or even when we don't yet see a better way but know something isn't working. Whether it's a marketing strategy, business process, or employee, if it isn't working, don't keep doing it. When a ship or rocket has a malfunction, they don't keep pushing forward with a broken component. Doing so will result in destruction and loss of life. Instead, they isolate and often shut down the system, sometimes even breaking it off. In this way, they are able to continue forward, rather than implode, explode, or sink.

Pufferfish Technique:

NEVER RELY ON WHAT'S ALWAYS BEEN
DONE TO JUSTIFY ANYTHING.

An Example of a Pufferfish

It is no secret that the airline industry has been in flux for decades. In 2014, Frontier Airlines® decided to launch its new marketing plan that included making the animals on their planes larger and more prominent. In an article by Denver's local 9News, one of the reasons cited for doing this included recognizing how important animals were to people and wanting to connect more with their client base. In fact, in 2016, Frontier® yielded to a year's worth of requests from 3rd and 4th grade students in the Denver area and put Marty the Marmot on one of their planes. This was a huge public relations event that involved the community while also promoting the refreshed brand of the company. The school principal said it was a great lesson for the kids in hard work, advocacy, and activism and thanked Frontier Airlines for helping them make an unforgettable memory.

In this example, Frontier Airlines used public involvement in a simple way to self-promote and participate in the community in a meaningful way. However, by also putting animals on the tail of their planes, they (purposefully or not) made themselves look bigger and more visible, just like a pufferfish.

Do you remember the last time you were on a plane? How about the last two times? Did you fly with the same carrier? I'm sure you didn't even think about which specific plane you were on, just what type of plane. By putting animal images on the planes, Frontier is drawing attention to the size of their fleet, rather than letting it be obscure. Do you know how many planes any carrier has? Do you care? Probably not, but if you fly Frontier, you will likely remember which animal was on your plane. You may even go look up, just like I did, how many planes they have and what animals adorn them. The animals have nothing to do with flight. In fact, they are only there for customer enjoyment. It is a simple, yet easy way to be seen, which is what their marketing department was going for. This is exactly what I want for you in your business.

The Steps to Being a Pufferfish

Now that you have reflected on the ways in which previous standards have held you back, I want you to take a look at what we did to be a Pufferfish. Use your fresh eyes to look at what each of these mean and think of the new ways you can implement them.

1. Do Good Work
2. Be a Networking Rockstar
3. Deliver Mind-Blowing Customer Service
4. Shamelessly Self-Promote

5. Give Back to the Community
6. Create a Star Team

That's all. The End. Just kidding.

They sound simple, and they are. However, most people think they are doing these things, and they either aren't doing them or aren't doing them effectively. We know they are effective when reality shows us they are. This means we are setting goals, tracking, and observing the results! Too often, business owners say they are doing something, but without tracking the results it's just action. They think they know what is happening, but they aren't tracking it to determine whether it is true and effective. Don't get me wrong, you do have an idea of what your business is doing, but without proper tracking, you don't really know. It's like trying to get somewhere based on the general direction, rather than the specific address.

Even in subjective fields like therapy, we are asked to quantify our results in order to show us our progress. We need to say something to the effect of: "I think I'm about a 4 on a scale of 10, and I'll know I'm successful when I'm at a 7." Why do therapists do that? They are helping you to quantify your results so you can determine if you've achieved them. Key Performance Indicators, or KPI's, need to be part of your everyday life, because while these 6 steps seem really simple, you will never know if they are effective, or if you have achieved them, if you don't have a way to measure the results.

Let's talk more about each step in general. The following chapters will go into more detail about each step and how we implemented them, so these are just overview concepts to get you thinking about what you might do and how you will know if you are successful.

Do Good Work

It doesn't matter how good your marketing and sales are if you don't do good work. In fact, I would even go as far as to say that doing good work is your BEST form of marketing. We have all heard a tale of a scammer. What makes them one? Usually, they don't perform the work they say they will. They don't do good work, and their reputation suffers for it.

There was a competitor in our market about a decade ago who touted themselves for outstanding customer service. Not only did they come fix your plumbing, they would pick up your morning newspaper and bring it in for you (among other things). Within a few years, they were out of business, despite having some of the highest profit in the industry. It was true that some people felt gouged by the prices – we'll talk about this again in a moment – but their complaints with the Better Business Bureau (BBB) weren't based on price, they were based on poor quality of work. It seemed their plumbers were better at delivering newspapers than they were at fixing leaks.

Back to price--remember in the beginning of this book, I mentioned that we knew we were entering a market with 950 competitors? Because of this, we understood we couldn't compete on price. Price should never be a motivating factor or differentiator in doing business even if you have always done it that way. If you want to last in business long term, and pay your bills, pricing must be based on the value you bring. If you can't sell based on value, you may want to look at business resources that will help you do so.

In order to do good work, you must set goals, track the results, and adjust until reality meets expectation. I'll share with you some of the ways we did this in the chapter, Do Good Work.

Be a Networking Rockstar

Being a networking rock star involves knowing what groups to join and showing up to them. Again, I need to tell you that if you aren't doing good work, networking is going to be painful. It is, after all, direct accountability to the community you serve. For example, if you network at BOMA (Building Owners and Managers Association), and do a terrible job once hired, you can expect that Property Manager will tell others, especially if you don't make it right. However, if you have nailed step one and are doing great work, that Property Manager will tell others, and they will likely keep their alliance with you even when management changes, or they change to a new building. After all, you made them look like a rock star for having a contact like you.

Being a networking rock star also requires setting a goal, tracking and observing the results. You need to know what your investment is into the networking organization and have a revenue goal you expect to gain. Then you have to be able to track whether or not it is meeting your expectations. One of the biggest mistakes I see business owners make is joining the wrong networking organizations. Trust me, you don't always know, but that's when it becomes a game to discover whether or not it is a fit. Also, there are certain clues to watch for before you join. We will talk about the questions you should ask before jumping into a networking organization as well as where to look for the ones that are best for you in the chapter on being a networking rock star.

Deliver Mind-Blowing Customer Service

Anyone who meets my husband typically walks away with a smile. He's friendly and cheery, like sunshine. I really mean this. He's also amazingly talented – a master plumber, a NATE-certified HVAC technician, and a boiler genius, as well as a thermal heat and solar tech. For those of you familiar with the DISC assessment, my husband is a high I. This makes him incredibly friendly, valuing relationships first, which makes him a natural at customer service, and a great role model and leader for our client-centric business.

When we became finalists in the Denver Better Business Bureau Torch Awards, one of the judges said of us: "Sunshine is a customer service company who happens to provide plumbing and heating." We went on to win a BBB Torch Award that year, and one of the best things that came of it was that quote. It proved to us that we did indeed live up to our plan to provide mind-blowing customer service. Our 12 Points of Love has become our checklist of what exactly we do to demonstrate our customer service which will be discussed more in its chapter as well.

We made customer service part of our culture by hiring staff who really understood what we were creating. We promoted our customer service success through a reputation management plan. Then, we put systems in place to capture social proof. According to whatis.techtarget.com, social proof is defined as: "the influence that the actions and attitudes of the people around us (either in real life or online) have on our own behavior."

We set criteria for specific actions, and this plan created and automated processes for each action so that everyone was on the same page, and customer service was easy to do. In the chapter on this topic, I will also address how competing on price is killing your business.

Shamelessly Self-Promote

Some people think I am joking when I say that I am a shameless self-promoter. I'm not joking. And frankly, it bothers me that others in business don't self-promote enough. If you aren't shamelessly self-promoting, what are you doing to grow your business? Are you sitting in a closet drawing vision boards and hoping clients magically dial your number, show up at your store, or type in your web address? I really hope not. If you are helping people by doing your job well, giving stellar customer service, and doing good things for your community, why wouldn't you let everyone know it? You wouldn't have anything to be ashamed of.

One of the ways we shamelessly self-promote is through the use of awards. We actively apply for awards, and in doing so, win a portion of them. This will be discussed in detail later, but it's important to know it was part of our plan from the beginning. It has been a very inexpensive way to get great public relations.

Have you heard of the concept of the Three Foot Rule? Wherever you go, when someone comes within three feet of you, you tell them what you do! Again I say, if you got into business thinking you wouldn't ever do sales or marketing and that shameless promotion isn't your thing, take my advice and get out now. The choice is yours.

Give Back to the Community

There are so many benefits to being a philanthropic organization, many of which we will discuss in this section's unique chapter. One of the biggest right now is that the Millennial workforce desires to work for a socially conscious employer. If you want a workforce and/or customers that fall in this generational group, then giving back to the community must be part of your strategic business plan.

Just like jaw dropping customer service is part of our culture, so is community give back. It is part of who we are, how we hire, and how we represent ourselves in our community.

How is community give back part of your culture, or is it? If not, how can it be implemented in a genuine way? What organizations do you support or would you want to support? How do they align with your business goals and vision?

When you think about community give back, consider what matters to you, your clients and your employees. We will cover all this in the chapter on community give back. KPI's in this area can include showing tangibly that you are indeed giving back in a strategic and meaningful way. Be precise in how you give and how much you give as well as how you leverage it in alignment with your overall business goals and reputation. This will be covered in more detail in the chapter for this point.

Create a Star Team

Having the best team takes work. Employees can take your business to new heights and can also be the hardest part about being in business. Often when it comes to employees there is a love/hate relationship. We love the support they bring; we hate hiring, firing and discipline. We love when customers delight over them and hate when they are a source of complaints. Finding the best team often comes through trial and error, mistakes and failures, magical successes, learning and re-writing, and most importantly, keeping the right mindset.

When employees are seen as, or expected to be, anything less than amazing and great, we can get into a place of treating them like poorly behaved children who don't deserve Christmas. However, when you love them, and I mean really, genuinely care for them, and show it, there are benefits. You will naturally hold them accountable, just like you do to your children or pets to keep them from running in the street and getting hit by a car. You will naturally find ways to help them be successful, like automating their redundant tasks and rewarding them for performance. You will hold on loosely and let them choose to leave if they aren't the right fit. And yes, your heart will even break sometimes when they do really stupid things.

Because we could write an entire book just on employees, in addition to having a chapter for employees, we have put a section in several other chapters titled, "A Note About Employees." This section will discuss the chapter topic in relationship to employees in order to keep it simple and connect the dots.

Are you ready to dive in deeper?

In the next few chapters we will dive deeper into each of the steps and the ways we've implemented them, messed them up, and found real success. Before we begin, here are some questions to ask, along with space for you to answer. I encourage you to not just glaze past them, but to really take time to consider them.

What areas of my business do I do simply because they are **the way they have always been** done? (Think about innovation here – how can you be a leader in your industry if you keep following the same rules?)

_____

_____

_____

_____

_____

What do I find myself complaining about over and over again? What am I holding in place simply because they have always been done that way?

_____

_____

_____

_____

_____

What do I wish I could change? More than just what you find yourself complaining about, what else do you wish you could change?

_____

_____

_____

_____

_____

Brainstorm some ways it could change – from outlandish to common. How could you disrupt your industry? How can you be a Purple Cow (the concept made popular by best-selling marketing guru Seth Godin)?

_____

_____

_____

_____

_____

Pufferfish Technique:

Take time to journal now about some areas of business where you may be able to innovate. What are areas in your business/industry that are **the biggest gripes** – whether from customers, employees, or vendors?

_____

_____

_____

_____

_____

Now, brainstorm some ways you may be able to overcome these gripes. Don't censor yourself – be as practical or silly as you'd like.

_____

_____

_____

_____

_____

In our industry, one huge gripe by employees was the requirement to work on-call hours. So, we changed it. (You'll read more about that in a future chapter.) A huge compliant from customers was that they had to wait for a technician to arrive for a quote. So, we changed that as well with Video Plumber®.

How often do you solicit feedback from your clients to see what complaint they have that you may be able to solve? When do you ask your employees about the problems they are seeing and what solutions you could offer? Take a moment to brainstorm how to implement a feedback loop.

When do you give yourself the time to **explore what could be**? Many business owners get stuck in working IN their business rather than ON it. If it is not part of your schedule to explore opportunities on a regular basis, do it now. Pick a day (weekly, monthly, quarterly and annually) to spend ONLY on working ON your business. Write down what you want to accomplish in each of these days.

For example:
Weekly: budgeting
Monthly: marketing opportunities – research what's new and where you may need to be to grow
Quarterly: what contests or PR opportunities are available?
Annually: Revisit vision, mission, goals, projections and more

What do you want to accomplish in your days when you work ON your business?

Weekly:

Monthly:

Quarterly:

Annually:

Am I willing to start thinking differently? Being willing to learn and try something new is the foundation of all growth. It allows you to have an open mind and consider what is possible rather than getting stuck in a place with limited options. Consider how different your choices are in a mall of stores rather than one store. When you are shopping at Ace Hardware®, you get hardware. When you shop at Mall of America, you get everything! (This question is rhetorical, but you can write "Yes!" if you'd like).

_____

_____

_____

_____

_____

What if I was the NEW CEO of my own company? Next Monday morning, I want you to walk into your office with new eyes. Pretend that you just bought YOUR company and take a hard, honest look at your business as it would be seen by an outsider. Evaluate every employee and their performance; you'll need to pretend that you aren't related to them, married to them or friends with them. BE HONEST. What do you see?

_____

_____

_____

_____

_____

Do I need support? Do you need a coach, a master-mind, or some other people or systems in place to help you with your new thinking, new goals and new systems? Take a moment to get specific about what you need help with. This will help you identify the right people to put in your life.

_____

_____

_____

_____

_____

2

Do Good Work

DOING GOOD WORK IS YOUR BEST FORM OF MARKETING. You can't retain customers or get referrals if you do sloppy work. You can't win awards, be a community leader or even show your face well on social media or at networking events if you don't first do good work.

When we first set out in business, we decided that we didn't want to be a 100-truck company. At the time of the writing of this book, we have a total of 17 employees. We aspire to be a 15-truck operation with an outstanding reputation, good profit margin and really happy employees. The bigger you get as a company, the harder it can be to keep employees happy and know what your customers want. So in many ways, we run like a mom and pop shop but focus on processes and procedures to create a consistent experience every time our customers engage with us. Being able to replicate the same outcome is key to meeting the requirement of doing good work. Let's revisit some of the questions I brought up in the first chapter:

- What does *doing good work* look like in your business?
- Do you have it clearly defined in ways that your employees and customers know what to expect?

If your employees clearly know what you expect, it allows you to hold them accountable to those expectations. It also means you can reward them for it. We find most frustrations between employers and employees have to do with a mismatch in expectations. However, there is no way that you can include every single expectation in an employee handbook, and even if you do, there is no way it will be read.

In our company, the implementation of this step included getting really clear about the absolutely most important things, and continuously driving them home. One way this is done is through adopting a set of values that the company stands for and the behaviors that fall under each value. For example, one company value could be 'respect', which is demonstrated through respect of employee and customer property. Expectations around this can clearly be defined as not leaving materials behind and cleaning your space to be as good as, or better than you found it. Values will encompass a larger, or global, concept, but how that value is played out is in line with your expectations and helps define the accountability and performance expectations.

Write what your expectations are around *doing good work*. Is this communicated to your staff? Your customers? Do your decisions line up with this?

For example, let's say your definition of doing good work is:

- Call every customer back within 4 hours

- Show up on time
- Clean up after yourself
- Leave the home better than you found it.

First, does your staff know that? Second, do they do it? How are they held accountable for following these expectations? Do your customers know to expect this of you? Would it help them to know it? Do you train and equip your staff to follow through with your expectations, or do they need to figure it out on their own? How can you better prepare them to meet your expectations, thereby allowing each person to do their job to the best of their ability? What can you take over to create a consistent experience so each staff member can provide the same standard of care to every client? This can include automation tools, or delegating tasks to a specific person or people.

Again, it all comes back to setting the goal then tracking and observing the results. If you want your staff to call a customer back within 4 hours, what's stopping that from happening now? Set the goal, track it to discover how it is or is not working, adjust and do it again. Continue to do this until every aspect of *doing good work* matches your expectations.

But how do you track it? Here's an example of a measurement tool we put in place to track the four goals mentioned above. The primary way we measure these components is through a customer survey that is automatically sent to each and every client immediately following their service call. In the survey we ask if they were called prior to the technician's arrival, if the tech was on time, if we cleaned up after ourselves, and if we satisfactorily solved their problem. If the client doesn't complete the survey, we call them a few days later and ask them. This phone call also opens the door for further feedback, which we can then address, and resolve, if needed.

When it comes to customer feedback, if you aren't asking for it, you won't be getting a complete picture of the type of service you are providing. Remember, most people won't leave a review or say what is good, or bad, unless they are asked.

When employees hear customer feedback, it reinforces good behavior and allows them to consider actions taken that were less than successful. It also allows for open communication and creates a culture for continuing improvement by bringing up situations, challenges, and training opportunities that may otherwise be swept under the rug. For example, it's one thing for a manager to say, "Don't leave a handprint on the customer's wall." It's entirely different when, at a staff meeting, the manager reads aloud the story of Mrs. Jones who was upset about the handprint on the wall and the manager can ask questions such as, "Do you have cleaning materials on your truck? What else can we do to make sure we aren't leaving handprints?"

The second scenario allows the employees to own the process and the solution to the problem, rather than just having it be passed down from management. It's empowering, and having an empowered staff results in better work, greater morale, and more problem solving. It also gives management the feedback they need to better equip their employees, in this case, by providing cleaning materials, and helping to build a process where the technicians check the work area before they leave.

By implementing an automatic survey, followed up by a phone call, we are able to track, and hold the technicians accountable to our expectations. From there, we use the feedback from the survey to help equip the staff to do a better job.

A Lesson From The Trenches

In the early stages of our business, we began to recognize we had little control over the customer experience because we were using subcontractors. We realized that we needed to transition to having employees, where we could manage how they interacted with our clients. Let me share with you how the whole process went, which was critical to the concept of Doing Good Work.

In our business' infancy, William was getting too busy to do all the work that was being called in. We decided to start using subcontractors to help us with the workload. The IRS cares deeply about the distinction between subcontractors and employees as it ties into how taxes are to be remitted. In our case, we controlled the subcontractor's hours, required them to follow our processes, provided training, and even issued them work trucks. The role of subcontractor versus employee was becoming more and more blurred. This could have set us up for an audit or even a lawsuit. We were requiring subcontractors to act like employees, but we weren't providing them with the benefits enjoyed by employees.

Our bookkeeper let us know that in addition to potentially facing IRS repercussions, we were significantly and negatively impacting our cash flow as 50% of our income, after parts and materials, was being paid out. We simply couldn't afford to continue using subcontractors. Not financially, not legally, not for our reputation, and not for our growth.

We approached our subcontractors and offered them the opportunity to become our employees. It was going to mean they'd have a steady paycheck and benefits. None of our subcontractors accepted our offer. In fact, one was so offended he threw the truck keys at us. They felt their compensation would be diminished, and they'd be better on their own – as owners of their own companies with all the freedom that allowed. Overnight, we went from a full queue of work and the means to handle it, to a very stressed and overworked single technician – William, my husband.

We starting running ads to hire, and slowly, we grew. As our business grew, we purchased a truck, stocked it and hired again. Finally, we were able to control costs and control quality. We interviewed for the traits we wanted and the culture we wanted to create. We trained them with our expectations, and we offered them benefits that built a Star Team. I use my straight-forward New Jersey personality to hold my team accountable. It doesn't always make me the most popular person, but it is always honest and to the point. Vendors and employees alike know exactly where they stand after a "New Jersey conversation" - it is effective and truthful, if not pretty.

It was not easy to move from subcontractors who made their own rules to employees who we held to our standards, but it was important. It is also one of the best moves we've made. Be prepared, that if you start your business, like many do, using subcontractors rather than employees, they may walk when you are ready to transition.

A Note About Employees

We've kissed a lot of frogs when it comes to employees, but we didn't give up. You live and learn and keep pushing forward, further refining what you are looking for, how it's delivered, and how you compensate for desired behaviors and more.

Because doing good work is placed in the hands of our employees, we treat them well. We offer what some call *crazy* benefits. There is a reason why we offer these, and part of it is to keep high quality employees. Employee turnover is a huge expense that many businesses feel but don't quantify. Some studies show employee turnover can cost up to twice the employee's annual salary. Think about how much time and effort goes into hiring and training a candidate, including the loss of production or production value that happens during training, and you can see how quickly costs can add up.

Doing good work requires clear expectations, tracking and adjusting. Do you equip your staff to follow through with the expectations you have given them? Do you make it easy to give clients a consistent experience? When it comes to consistency, it starts with setting a goal, tracking it, seeing where and how you are falling short, adjusting, and then repeating this over and over. If you continue to do this, you will find where your processes have holes, and you will create long-lasting outcomes. But remember if it stops working or is no longer a priority, don't keep doing it just because you always have. Keep growing and innovating to stay fresh and in alignment with your changing goals.

Are you ready to dive in deeper?

Let's take some time to dive into the questions we asked earlier in the chapter.

WHAT DOES *DOING good work* look like in your business? Be specific.

_____

_____

_____

_____

_____

HOW CAN you communicate these expectations to current and future staff?

_____

_____

. . .

_____

_____

HOW CAN you communicate these expectations to customers?

_____

_____

_____

_____

_____

IS THERE anyone else who needs to understand what doing good work looks like in your business?

_____

_____

. . .

DO this for each position in your company. Talk to your front-line employees as well as management to define them further. As your business grows, you may want to consider future positions and how you'd like them to look as well. Take time now to make an organizational chart so you can determine what you want from planned, anticipated staff.

3

Be a Networking Rockstar

WHEN BUSINESS OWNERS FIRST START THEIR BUSINESSES, they have a tendency to be 100% involved in day-to-day operations. They make the mistake of positioning themselves as a 'technician' as explained in *The eMyth* by Michael Gerber. In order to have a successful business, you need to be out in the community, not chained to a desk. Your primary role should be in sales, not in operations.

Networking for your business helps you to establish trust within the communities you are involved in. It forms important professional connections and creates spheres of influence as well as providing accountability and word-of-mouth advertising. If you are a new business owner, it also helps you learn more about business as you begin to build circles of peers who are entrepreneurs, managers and salespeople.

Start by making a plan for networking. Look at who your ideal clients are and where you can locate them. Look at your community and what organizations align best with your mission, vision and business philosophies.

To Determine If a Group or Organization is a Good Fit

As you begin to look at your options for networking, it's important to consider these questions:

- Are my ideal clients in this group?
- Is the financial investment likely to be recouped?
- How long until I will see a return on investment?
- How much business will I need to get from the group to make it financially responsible?
- What is the time commitment?
- Do I have the time to commit to this organization or is there someone else on my team who can?
- If so, is this in their skill set?
- When (if ever) do I bring on a salesperson for this role?
- What goals do I have for this group in terms of leveraging my position? (For example, do I want to speak to the group, serve on a board, lead a committee, attend events, etc. You must know your goal in order to reach it.)
- Are my goals within the organization realistic and achievable (i.e., will the organization ever let me speak, or do they only hire third party presenters)?

Here are some suggestions on the types of groups and organizations you may look into for networking:

Chamber of Commerce

Your local Chamber of Commerce can be a great ally in your business development. They tend to offer benefits to their members including a ribbon cutting to kick off your business, networking opportunities, community education, business benefits and more. The Chamber that covers your business location will help you meet those in your community who can become great power partners (people to exchange referrals with), as well as vendors for your business needs.

Sometimes your local Chamber isn't a good fit, and you may want to look at other Chambers that better align with your business. For example, we also joined the Women's Chamber as that allowed us to better connect with our ideal demographic. Additionally, we joined a Chamber that had a subgroup of contractors that allowed us to build deeper relationships with companies we work beside on various projects.

Lead Groups

Your Chamber likely offers a lead group, and you can join that as well as look at other area lead groups. Organizations such as BNI, LeTip, and other regional networking groups offer training, skill building and connections that will help you grow both personally and professionally.

Industry Specific Associations

Industry specific associations such as apartment associations, restaurant associations, BOMA, or groups specifically designed for your industry are very helpful. Groups exist for a number of industries such as HR, tourism, construction trades and more. These groups can offer political lobbies for your causes, accreditation and certification, and significant professional connections and support.

Service Organizations

Community service groups such as Optimists, Kiwanis or Rotary can offer ways to meet other connected people while also giving back. Check out what is available in your area, as well as who is involved in the group to make a determination about joining.

Conventions

Conventions are often short-term events put on by one of the above organizations. They are great for networking, especially if you are in a role that positions you as a speaker. Being a speaker, or in any leadership role for that matter, gives you and your business even more exposure while also affirming you as an industry leader, expert, or at least an influencer.

Regardless of the group or groups you join, these tips are critical:

1. Show up. If you can't make the time commitment to attend meetings, as well as get to know the members better, don't join.
2. Participate. Don't expect to show up and get business. Networking is about relationships, so spend time to build them.
3. Track results. While you shouldn't expect new business on day one, you should be watching to see if you are getting financial rewards from your membership. (More about this later.)
4. Understand your visibility makes you known.

On this last point, I have to share a story.

I was at a convention and made a poor decision to drink more than I should have. I didn't dance on the bar top, but pretty close. Basically, I made an ass of myself in front of people I admired. When you network, it's important to know that you are purposely making yourself visible. I think this is a big reason why most business owners don't network; they are afraid of speaking in public, want some level of anonymity, or consider themselves to be too shy or introverted. Being visible can be hard sometimes -- it opens you up to criticism, but it also keeps you accountable; it makes you vulnerable, but it also builds your credibility. Networking makes you a Pufferfish. When you network, you are putting yourself out into a sea of prospective clients and lead sources. It is the cheapest form of advertising as it increases your name recognition while also creating powerful relationships, and therefore it is worth the risk. Get over being shy and get out and network! And don't get drunk.

Pufferfish Technique:

TRACK EVERYTHING AND ADJUST BASED ON THE RESULTS

The Importance of Tracking

Sometimes I hear from coaching clients or people at conventions that networking doesn't work. Often I find that it isn't that it doesn't work, but rather that tracking isn't happening. One of our company's core values is Accountability. Tracking is a form of accountability as it watches the behavior of an activity to determine if it is performing as expected. Tracking is a crucial part of your marketing plan and must be implemented to evaluate your networking and all your forms of marketing.

Make a plan that lays out who you expect to reach, how much time and money you are expected to invest, any goals for a leadership role, and, most importantly, a tracking number to accurately gauge your return on investment. I learned that I could easy network full-time. I tried it all, and then I started tracking phone numbers specifically assigned to each organization. Each client in my database has a drop-down menu listing all the potential lead sources. When the client calls in on a tracked number, it will auto-populate. When it doesn't, my staff is required to ask how the lead found us. We look at these reports on a regular basis to determine their effectiveness.

These two strategies--assigning tracking numbers and requiring staff to ask the lead source--give me an accurate way to calculate our return on investment, which is critical for profit and for determining where my time is best spent. If I don't realize a 200% return, I don't continue investing in the organization. This means if I spent $1,000, I need to get $2,000 back in leads, or I cut the group. My time, skills and business are too important to waste on endeavors that don't generate income.

The other important component to this was understanding what my average ticket was so I could determine how many jobs I would need in order to hit my desired return. This helped guide my decision-making such as whether I felt sponsoring a $10,000 table at a one-time event would yield the approximately 26 jobs needed to break even, or 52 to achieve the profit I desired. This math and mentality became a compass for what to invest, or not invest in.

If you don't already have the technology in place or are unable to invest in it, consider putting together a simple spreadsheet or table for your clerical staff to complete. In one column, put the name of the event or marketing being offered. In the next column, leave enough space for a check or tick mark. In the next column, place the client's name or other identifier so you can keep track of the income that is generated. Finally, go back after the work has been done and assign a dollar amount to the client and the corresponding referral source.

This strategy can be implemented immediately to help

you start collecting data to make informed networking and marketing decisions. It is time to stop making excuses about not knowing where your marketing money is going and how it is performing.

Being Away From the Office

In all my networking and organization commitments outside the office, I am often asked how I am able to stay away from the office so much. The answer is that we are a fully digital, paperless company. All the information I need about my day-to-day operations is available to me through technology. I can look at any client, job, KPI, truck location, etc., by accessing the internet. In today's world this means checking my smart phone or taking my tablet or laptop into a nearby WiFi spot.

From the very beginning, we set up our company to be paperless. We invested in technology that from the start created efficiency, and therefore profitability.

A Note About Employees

We found that sometimes sending our employees to networking events worked, and sometimes it didn't. When thinking about using staff to network your business, consider some of the lessons we have learned.

First, we found the most effective networkers will be in a management or sales role. Managers are tied to outcomes and success - such as wanting employees to meet a certain quota or customer service rating. Because of this, they like the accountability networking provides since it creates an opportunity for feedback. When one of their peers in the networking group hires the company, that person will often let the manager know how it went - good or bad. This then allows the manager to praise what is working well, and make meaningful changes when needed. Networking can then create a natural feedback loop for more informed management.

Be supportive and go with them to the first networking meeting so you can see how they interact, as well as demonstrate your expectations. Watch their demeanor and ask for feedback; treat networking as if it's a new job because in essence it is. Don't send managers who have a debilitating fear of speaking or struggle with accountability or honesty (hopefully you don't have them on your team). Many managers will say they don't like groups or public speaking, but they can really grow and develop in a lead group. However, if they are petrified to speak, don't send them networking. By petrified, I mean they really can't speak in public--they freeze or just aren't social. Do everyone a favor and choose someone else.

For salespeople, networking is a natural and expected part of the role. Set up compensation to incentivize the results you want, and make sure they clearly understand your goals for each group. Be supportive of their efforts by listening to their feedback whether it is about something that didn't go well or suggestions for new opportunities. You should also provide them with tools to help them, such as business cards or giveaway gifts. Plan regular meetings to discuss their progress and challenges.

We have seen managers and technicians both get the itch to become their own boss when they see the success networking can bring. For this reason, I urge you not to use technicians, and to choose trustworthy managers who are invested in the success of the company, not their own pocketbook.

We have found that technicians and clerical staff aren't as successful in networking, because they don't have purchasing power or sufficient authority to make changes. Remember, most of the other people at the networking events have decision-making ability in their businesses. They are able to choose a new vendor for printing or telecom, or when they need help with financial planning or training their dog. It is a disservice to all involved if the person who is networking is unable to give referrals back to the networking group because they lack authority to do so. If you choose this route, discuss how referrals are to be given, especially if your company has representatives in several groups. For example, if you have 5 people networking on behalf of your company, create a rule that personal referrals are allowed, but not business ones. This may mean your staff person can refer themselves to the painter, but can't ask the painter for a bid on your building without your permission.

This may seem like a silly point, but if you consider it on a bigger scale, you may be facing five appointments a week with insurance agents, financial planners, IT professionals, website designers, printers, and others who all want to talk to a decision maker to sell their services. A chain of priority needs to be in place to be fair to your employees, their groups, and you.

And again, as always, track the results of the groups as well as the staff person's performance. If it isn't working, stop investing time and money into it. No more spending a dollar to make a dime! Invest in networking and watch your dollar become two, or more.

Are you ready to dive in deeper?

Let's take some time to dive into the questions we asked earlier in the chapter.

What organizations or groups have you looked into in the past?

_____

_____

_____

_____

_____

_____

Did they work? Why or why not?

_____

_____

_____

_____

Which would you like to look into now?

_____

_____

_____

_____

_____

How will you track your results?

_____

_____

_____

_____

_____

Who can help? (ie. a salesperson, member of management, etc.)

_____

_____

_____

Pufferfish Technique:

_____

_____

Remember to go back to the beginning of the chapter and answer those questions as well for each organization or group you check into.

4

Deliver Mind-Blowing Customer Service

COMPETING ON PRICE IS KILLING YOUR BUSINESS; COMPETE on customer service instead. Remember when I said that we had hundreds of competitors in our market and knew we couldn't compete on price? (I have said this before, but I'm saying it again because it is SO important.) Too many business professionals try to compete on price, and this is a mistake. No one has your business, even if there are thousands in your industry. No one has your skill set, even if there are tens of thousands of people with your job title. What you offer is unique, and therefore how you set your price is unique. Look at your goals and budget to set your prices, not to the competition. Anyone can survey competitors and many do, only to discover the RANGE of pricing that exists in their market. Pricing is a business tactic, you already know this. Some use low prices as a way to get a foot in the door. Others offer low prices and lower service levels. Some use high prices as a way to only appeal to high-end clientele and then provide services to keep those clients. It's all strategy, it is not based on what the market will bear. YOU determine what YOUR market will bear.

What are your goals, and what do your clients need to pay in order for you to meet those goals? What do you need to provide in order to get THOSE clients? This is the heart of customer service.

Customer service is knowing your clients and meeting their needs. Excellent customer service is knowing your clients so well that you empathize with them and create a *wow* experience.

The first time we were a finalist for the Better Business Bureau Torch Award (2016), we were honored to have one of the judges say of us:

"Sunshine is a customer service company who happens to do plumbing and heating."

This **PROVED** to us that our strategy to compete on service, not price, was evident and working. In fact, to create a *wow* experience for our clients, as well as to communicate to staff what our expectations are in regards to customer service, we came up with the Sunshine 12 Points of Love. Since I am a speaker and mention them frequently, these are becoming famous. They aren't magic. In fact, you probably have your 12 points, 7 steps, or whatever it is in your customer service strategy as well. We just documented it and share it like crazy! Seriously, sit down and think about your points and document them. Then be prepared to train your team to fulfill every one of them. Then, let your customers know about it every chance you get. I will share the points, then share how we do them, and how to make them work in and outside the service industry.

1. Answer the phone with "How can we make you smile today?"
2. Send an appointment reminder
3. Send a bio and picture of the technician
4. We don't use paper--everything is electronic
5. Follow-up with email immediately
6. Follow-up by phone within two days
7. Follow-up every month with specials and promos
8. Send Thank You notes - always
9. Send gifts at certain spend amounts
10. Send boo-boo gifts if we screw up
11. Have dog biscuits on the truck
12. Put clients in a hotel if we can't fix the problem right away

Pufferfish Technique:
DOCUMENT WHAT YOU ARE DOING AND SHARE IT LIKE CRAZY

Answer the Phone with "How can we make you smile today?"

Whether it's our in-office dispatch or our answering service, our phones are always answered with this question. It is also the Sunshine tagline, driving home our overall objective. If you don't have a tagline to use, consider creating one. It pauses the customer's automatic response and, in our case, we often get a laugh from them, already causing the smile.

A simple online search of "answering the phone with a smile" will bring up several articles stating that answering the phone with a smile can actually be perceived. Why not encourage clerical staff to get out of their standard routine of stating the business name alone and create a welcoming environment as soon as the client calls?

Solopreneurs or smaller teams can also use technology to help sort their calls. This creates a consistent experience for callers which produces a professional image as well as a Pufferfish Effect.

Send an Appointment Reminder

We use a dispatch program that allows us to collect our client's email address when they call. We use this email address in several steps of our 12 Points of Love, and one of those ways is to send an emailed appointment reminder. This sets a standard of communication so our clients understand we will be contacting them this way in the future. It also allows us to automate some of our processes, such as sending all customer email reminders out at specific intervals prior to our arrival.

Whether or not you are in a service industry, sending an appointment reminder is a way to create another touchpoint with your prospective client and increase the likelihood they will show up for the appointment, rather than leave you hanging. If you've ever sat for 10 minutes in a coffee shop after a 20-minute commute, you appreciate knowing well in advance if your appointment is a no-show. If you pay a gas bill on a fleet, you understand the value of this confirmation step as well.

Send a Bio and Picture of The Technician

The software we use to collect client data, including their email address, also allows us to specify which technician is assigned to their job. An email is automatically sent when the technician is assigned (or changed) that includes a pre-written bio of a few sentences such as name, how long with our company, how long in the industry, and maybe some personal information such as the city he/she lives in.

This feature is a game changer in the service industry where the technician will be going to the client's home. Because the majority of our clients are female, this is also a safety feature that gives them confidence in knowing WHO to expect when the doorbell rings.

Outside of the service industry, consider sending your picture in your email communication prior to meeting your client. Realtors® are great at putting their picture on just about every piece of communication they produce. Not only does this build rapport (people like to see a happy face), it helps you be identifiable when there is a face-to-face meeting, building confidence in the person who is meeting you.

We Don't Use Paper--Everything is Electronic

We decided to be paperless from the start, which meant we needed to find a technology-based solution to manage everything we would need for forms, communication and processes. Because we started this way, we never had to convert invoices to digital, worry about missing information (we mandated it in the form fields), or deal with wasteful redundancy.

There are people who cringe at the idea of being paperless. Others have grown to love the idea because of the ease it creates. Working with someone in business process management can help you to see your processes and what could become more streamlined both digitally and tangibly. For Sunshine, being paperless:

- Allows us to provide price quotes on the spot, and in writing, directly to the customer's email.

This overcomes the objection of needing more information or needing to consult with another person in the financial decision-making, because it's at their own fingertips to share with whomever they choose, such as a spouse.

- Helps our parts manager. When quotes are given, the line items are listed so our buyer knows exactly what parts are needed for the job when it sells.

- Helps us communicate more directly with staff. Depending on the urgency, we use text, email or phone to stay in touch with our employees. They use the same methods to contact the office. This allows the office to stay abreast of information from the field while eliminating the need for paper copies to be returned to the office.

- Helps us stay in touch with our clients because we collect their email addresses 100% of the time. This builds our client list allowing us to send them newsletters, important news, job information and more.

- Reduces the need for file cabinets. How much money is spent on endless file cabinets? We have just a few in our office, which saves us space for other things, such as conference tables so we can all see each other during office meetings.

Have you heard the expression, "There's an app for that"? It's true, with today's technology, it's easy to be paperless. Drag and drop technology helps you quickly create a myriad of solutions – you just need to ask. The time and money that you save can be better used to create higher levels of customer service through efficiency and automation.

Follow-Up With Email Immediately

Again, our software system automatically generates a follow-up email when the job is marked closed. This gives the client our contact information should they need to get in touch with us and also prompts them to complete a survey.

Obtaining reviews is one of our biggest Pufferfish Effect strategies. We currently have THOUSANDS of reviews online. This raises our rankings in online searches which helps clients and prospective clients find us, gives us valuable resources for testimonials and awards, and basically sells our services for us by creating **social proof -** the idea that the actions and feelings of our peers have an effect on our own behaviors and thoughts. Consider how often you read reviews and how they have impacted your decision whether or not to work with a particular business.

As part of our customer service strategy, we implemented a review system for customers and incentivized staff for positive reviews. Staff who don't do good work, don't get good reviews, and because we ask 100% of our customers for feedback (not just a select few), work that doesn't meet our standards never falls through the cracks. We have also tied our reviews to our technicians' bonus plan. If they don't get at least five excellent (5-star) reviews per month, they can't earn their bonus, end of story! Our outstanding customer service has become our marketing plan as it builds our reputation and increases word of mouth referrals.

Pufferfish Technique:
MAXIMIZE REVIEWS

Consider this: if 10% of your customers left 4- or 5-star reviews, how big would your company look? Take your average number of sales per week and multiply it by 10% - how many reviews would you have at the end of a year? How many reviews do your competitors have?

Reviews are a huge part of our business and our follow-up emails are designed to collect them. In your business, how are you following up with clients? Are you proactively soliciting feedback and reviews? If not, you should develop a way to do this with every customer.

Follow-Up by Phone Within Two Days

While an email is automatically generated when the job is completed, a personalized call is made to every client two days after the job is complete. When a technician leaves the job, everything is in working order. Two days later, the homeowner could have discovered something unsatisfying, such as a dirty handprint on the wall or that the handle fell off a faucet. We want to know these things so we can fix them right away. We want to be proactive and retain the client by letting them know our ears are open to their concerns. The last thing we want is for a customer to have a less than stellar experience and never tell us about it. As a result they might never call us again, or even worse, tell others about their poor service.

How many times have you had a poor customer service experience? It may have been at a restaurant or when you called a service provider with a problem and received mediocre service. It wasn't bad enough to complain about, so you didn't, but you vowed to not use them again. When asked by a friend or family member, you likely discouraged them from using that company, maybe even going as far as telling them the story of your experience.

Let's face it, some people are just not complainers. They may prefer to avoid conflict. Maybe they don't want to be seen as negative or a complainer, but they create negativity for your company by not being a fan or supporter. When you proactively reach out to these people, they will give you an honest answer, even though they wouldn't call to complain. These are detractors, and by asking their opinion, you allow them to be heard, and it allows you to step up your customer service by addressing their concerns.

Follow-up Every Month with Specials and Promos

Every month we send out an email newsletter with specials, promotions and any additional information about the company that we feel creates value for our clients. We also give them information about ways to save money, make better buying choices, learn about their plumbing and heating from a practical standpoint, and more. Every single one of our customers, because they provide their email address when they call us for service, is on our list and of course, has the choice to opt-out at any time. This newsletter creates an ongoing touch to keep us on their mind since we don't have the type of service they need every week, every month or even yearly.

An email newsletter should create value for the reader, not simply be an ongoing sales pitch. We maximize our newsletter by promoting our blog and social media, and invite the readers to follow us on social media for additional tips and information. Remember every time you create content you can reuse it in a variety of ways. As a coach I see clients spinning their wheels to produce, produce, produce, when they could just better maximize what they already have. Our social media, blog and website all work together to build a big and consistent presence. They are all designed as customer touchpoints to help them remember us and to keep us relevant to our clients. In addition, the frequency and consistency of our posts makes us look much larger than we are, creating a Pufferfish Effect. We've partnered with a few technology and marketing companies who make this process simple and efficient.

If you were to consider your newsletter as an extension of your customer service, how might it look differently?

Send Thank You Notes - Always

Since we provide service at our customer's home, we have the benefit of having their address in addition to their email address. Every month, we send branded Thank You cards to that month's clients. The cards are all the same, but are individualized with the customer's name. We use a service that automatically addresses the cards and sends them on our behalf, making our labor minimal. The art of Thank You cards, real cards with postage affixed and no sales pitch, has been lost. We feel this is an important part of customer service that is unexpected and provides a *wow* factor, and it certainly isn't something our competitors are doing!

Are you sending Thank You notes? How could you do this? Would it improve your customer service levels to do so?

Send Gifts

In addition to sending cards, we choose to send gifts to clients when they have spent a certain amount of money in one month with our company- typically at the level of a new water heater or furnace. The client is not aware of this practice, it is just something we do. When they receive the gift, they are often surprised. It is likely they didn't receive gifts from other service providers, so this makes us stand out. The gifts we give are usually less than 10% of what the customer spent, and it is only on our highest ticket items.

With this point of love, we did need to practice with a few options before finding what worked best for us. For a time, we purchased supplies and assembled the gifts at the office and then hand-delivered them. If the client wasn't home, we would leave the gift on the doorstep. We learned this wasn't a very good idea, so we found a service that would safely deliver gifts on our behalf.

Gifts should not be something customers expect – they should just show up. When you offer a free gift included with an offer, that is expected by the customer and is "trumpeted" or announced. A gift as a part of customer service should be covert, although you may see a client share about it. You might even decide to say you are delivering gifts without providing more detail.

Are gifts part of your customer service? How might you be able to incorporate that into your business model? What rules would you need to put in place to make it happen?

Send Boo-Boo Gifts if We Screw Up

Less than 1% of the time we make mistakes that aren't remedied with a simple call to the customer. When this happens, we send an apology in the form of a gift. One example of this was when had to cancel an appointment with a customer because an emergency came up for the assigned technician and we didn't have someone else to send. We rescheduled for the next convenient date for the customer, and sent flowers as an apology. We understand that waiting for a service technician to fix something in your home isn't the most pleasant scenarios. When we weren't able to follow through on the appointment time, and we aren't saying bumping them a few hours but rather an entire day, we knew that was a huge disruption for them. We felt it was only appropriate to thank them for their flexibility. After all, they had hundreds of other plumbers in the area they could have called, but they were willing to wait for us, and we don't take that lightly.

Have Dog Biscuits on the Truck

Having dog biscuits on every service truck allows us to show kindness to the furry family members of our clients. We understand how important pets are, not just to our clients, but our staff as well. This is a tangible way we can show it.

Put Clients in a Hotel if We Can't Fix the Problem Right Away

Yes, we really do. This may sound outrageous, and it is, but it delivers the type of outstanding customer service we want to be known for. We have only had to do this a few times over the years, but it has made a huge impact when we've done it. We weren't able to fix an air conditioner one very hot summer day, so we put a mom and child up in a hotel for the night. Were they upset with us for not being able to get them service? Not at all. In fact, they were happy to stay another day and enjoy the hotel pool while we continued the installation of their new unit.

So, when it comes to providing excellent customer service, how do you feel you do? Are you known for it? What would it take for you to be known for it? What strategy can you implement immediately? What other steps should you put in place to establish or solidify your company as a customer service company first and foremost?

Are you ready to dive in deeper?

Let's take some time to dive into the questions we asked earlier in the chapter.

What are you already doing as part of your customer service that can be better documented and shared?

_____

_____

_____

_____

_____

What's your company tagline or motto? Does it clearly communicate your overall objective?

_____

_____

_____

_____

Pufferfish Technique:

How can you create a consistent "appointment reminders"? If it's not applicable, what else can you do to create a touchpoint with clients before meetings?

_____

_____

_____

_____

_____

What systems, software, apps or automation might you put into place to help improve your customer experience?

_____

_____

_____

_____

_____

What do you have in place to follow up with 100% of your clients? What needs to change to make this happen?

_____

_____

_____

_____

_____

What do you have in place to capture reviews and/or testimonials from 100% of your clients? Remember, you won't
have a 100% response, but by asking all your clients, you
can expect to get about 10% back. The more you get, the
bigger you look!

_____

_____

_____

_____

_____

What do you have in place to consistently nurture clients?
How often do they hear from you and by what method(s)?
What changes do you need to make to have this happen?

_____

_____

_____

_____

Pufferfish Technique:

What type of thank you do you offer? What qualifications (if any) do clients need to have in order to get a gift? Are there levels? How will gifts be sent? Will clients be told ahead of time about the gifts or not?

_____

_____

_____

_____

What 'wow' can be put in place for when you make a mistake?

_____

_____

_____

_____

What other special treats can be put in place to wow clients?

_____

_____

_____

_____

5

Shamelessly Self-Promote

I LIKE TO TALK ABOUT SHAMELESS SELF-promotion directly following the entire chapter on customer service, and here's why, anyone can shamelessly self-promote only to have it fall on deaf ears. If you toot your own horn, and no one is around to applaud, it's quite sad. However, if you are patting yourself on the back and others join in and start praising you too, it is incredibly satisfying. When you provide stellar, outlandishly fantastic customer service, you have no reason for shame. And you will also find your customers are shouting your praises, so tell others about it! This is a huge part of being a Pufferfish!

Did you go into business thinking you wouldn't ever do sales or marketing? If so, save yourself the pain of business ownership right now and either become a silent partner or find a job. That sounds meaner than I intend. This is a great time and place to introduce Aunt Frankie. Aunt Frankie is my mom's sister. We are only eight years apart in age, so she has always been more of a sister to me than an aunt. When you think of a stereotypical wealthy, confident and beautiful New Jersey woman, that would be Aunt Frankie. And she is a hoot!

One time, at the height of a recession, I was having a really hard time financially. I was trying to run my coaching business in Breckenridge, Colorado and when the market dropped, I quickly lost every single customer. I called Aunt Frankie for a pep talk, but instead, I received something much more valuable....a Jersey Lesson that went something like this:

"Susan. Susan, put down the phone and go get a raaaaaggggg. (that would be a rag if it wasn't in her NJ accent). Go get a raaaaggggg, Susan. When you have it, pick up the phone.

I promptly did. "Ok Auntie, I have it, now what?"

"Now reach down there and polish off those brass balls you have and go out and make a sale. You are a phenomenal salesperson and a great coach, so go make it happen".

There it is. Straight shooting, NJ motivation. That is also how I lead. Please understand, that when I talk about being shameless, I don't mean doing something unethical or even out of alignment with who you are. What I am saying is that if you've really set up your business to be successful and truly in service of others, then promoting it becomes your mission. You have the confidence to be brassy and proud of what you've created and the people you serve. Shameless self-promotion becomes a joy, not a burden. You begin to shout from mountain tops because you know the good you are doing.

Women especially tend to be humble and don't promote themselves the way they should. Here are some questions to consider to help you overcome this humility:

How often do you leave the house without business cards on you or in your car? Are you always ready to share your *elevator pitch*? Can you engage in the Three

Foot Rule? Are you ashamed of your business? If so, why and how can you change that? Is it a mindset issue about money or greed that needs to be addressed? Are you afraid of sales or your sales skill set? What is your sales process? What is your marketing strategy? Have you ever considered leveraging awards to increase your exposure?

It's hard to be humble when you are so dang proud of what you've built. It's hard to NOT self-promote when you are already being touted as the next best thing to sliced mozzarella from the clients you are serving. As part of our marketing strategy, we leveraged awards. Applying for awards is part of our public relations and an important part of our brand.

Pufferfish Technique:
APPLY FOR AWARDS

Some of Sunshine's awards include (as of the publication of this book):

- 5-year Angie's List Super Service Award Winner
- *Denver Business Journal* #1 Fastest Growing Company 2015, 2016, 2017, 2018
- *Denver Business Journal* Small Business of the Year 2016, 2017
- Service Titan "Titan of the Month" for outstanding growth
- Colorado Companies to Watch Winner 2016
- *Denver Business Journal* Top 100 Women-Owned Companies 2016, 2017
- *Denver Business Journal* Best Places to Work 2017
- Better Business Bureau Torch Award for Business Ethics 2017
- *PHC News* Contractor of the Year 2017
- North Metro Chamber Small Business Person of the Year 2018

- CampExperience™ Network "Women Who Rock" 2017

Here's how you can do this as well.

What Matters To Your Customer?

We chose our demographic, and therefore knew them well. We didn't focus on Property Managers or Realtors® (although we got them too); we focused on middle- to upper-class women. We looked at a variety of awards, as well as who was sponsoring them and took into consideration what mattered to our target demographic. Middle- to upper-class women care about us being on Angie's List, in the BBB, and in the *Denver Business Journal.* They care that we are a woman-owned business because they associate that with an understanding that they want technicians who are nice, friendly, and clean (no rude, plumber-crack, condescending dirt-balls).

Winning an award from the CampExperience™ Network was a huge confirmation that we are indeed making an impact with our target market – it is exclusively made up of our demographic, and is one of the awards that we didn't self-nominate. It was an incredible honor because it was a perfect example of being recognized in a way that mattered to our primary customer.

What Matters To The Award?

Each award has specific criteria that need to be met in order to be eligible. Research the awards that exist and determine if you qualify. For example, if you have been in business 3 years and the award requires 10 years, don't apply. I know it may sound silly to put it that way, but there are some awards a bit less obvious than others in this regard.

Also, find awards that align with your business, don't just go after any of them. For example, if you are woman-owned, look at whether that matters to your potential clients. Does it create new opportunities for you or not? Find awards that will highlight what is unique about your business, reinforce your company values, and build credibility with your target demographic.

Do you want to toot your own horn in the area of ethics? Sustainability? Customer service? How do you run your company that supports that currently? What can you improve to demonstrate it even further?

When you begin filling out these applications for awards, you will start to see the holes that exist between the beliefs you have and the actions your company takes. For example, if you say that your company values community give back, be prepared to show what you do to support that idea. Consider getting an application for an award you would like to have in the future. Then, use the questions on the application to adjust your business goals to better exemplify the award's primary objectives, truly changing the company for the better (not just paying lip-service for the sake of the award).

What Matters To Your Employees?

This is an important one, especially as we see more and more Millennials joining our companies. This generation wants to feel like they are part of a bigger picture. They want connection and transparency. As with any population, you can't please everyone and should never make a blanket assumption, however, like your demographic, they likely have commonalities that create a pattern of interest. And if you don't know, ask them. You, as the head of your company, can also create the culture that others function within. We have found that employees who don't fit our culture simply self-select out, leaving us with those who do resonate with the things that collectively matter.

So, create a culture or define the interest and search for awards that are attractive in this arena. For us, we won the Denver Business Journal Best Places to Work 2017 award in part because of our robust employee benefits.

Once you have determined WHAT awards to apply for, apply for them! The main difference between those who win awards and those who don't, is that they didn't apply. That old adage "You have not because you ask not" is true! Apply.

Above, I hinted about one of the really great things about applying. Even in applying, you are helping your business to be better than it currently is because the practice of articulating why you deserve an award helps you to:

1. **Own it**

Owning it means that you really take responsibility for your business and where it is today. You are staking a claim, in essence saying, "I've worked for this and I deserve this."

2. **Grow into it**

Grow into it means that you give yourself an opportunity to reflect on your business and discover the gaps between reality and your desired outcome and then work to fix them. For example, you may begin to see that while you tout customer service, you really don't do much more than answer the phone and show up on time. You may also see that you don't mention much in your marketing about community give back, but you support youth sports, donate to a charity fundraiser every year, and clean up litter in your neighborhood. This can be a very empowering practice.

3.**Put the blood and sweat into it**

What I mean here is again in the course of completing the application, you go through a process that you begin to take control of. It takes work to do some of these applications – the Better Business Bureau Torch award application was over 30 pages the first year we applied and over 50 the second year. We took it seriously, as we should, because the judges take their role very seriously. If doing the application doesn't spark a fire of passion in your belly, then you either don't have a passion for your business or for the award. However, if the problem is that you just hate filling them out, then you can hire someone to do it for you.

Remember this is part of your marketing plan. Instead of investing money into advertising, you are investing time into the application process. Treat it as though you are investing thousands into an advertising campaign.

4.**Learn perseverance**

Let's face it, you aren't going to win every award you apply for. Sometimes, you will just shrug it off, holding onto hope for the next one. Other times, you will be a finalist and not win, which can be discouraging. However, being a finalist is still public relations worthy. When you get into a mentality of being an award winner, losses don't hurt as much. Just keep trying.

Submitting for awards that you are qualified to win is only a numbers game before you become a finalist and/or winner. You then want to position this with the media and in your marketing. Submit your award status to trade publications, Chambers of Commerce, and anywhere that news can be submitted. Be sure to share it to your social media channels as well. You can hire a public relations specialist to assist you, or ask a staff person who is savvy with online matters to help you submit your news. Start with publications you subscribe to or run ads with – they are usually happy to help and are a warm contact.

A Note About Employees

When you win awards, your employees also get a sense of pride in the company they work for, especially when they feel the award is earned because they understand the work that has gone into it. It builds confidence in a staff person to tell people their company won an award for ethics, for example. Your staff then get even more buy-in than they had before about why working for you is valuable. Your awards can even become a retention and recruiting device for top talent in your industry.

When you have employees excited to work for you, that also shows through in their work performance and when they are dealing with customers. Consider awards that really feature the qualities of your business – all aspects of it – that you want to be known for.

Are you ready to dive in deeper?

Let's take some time to dive into the questions we asked earlier in the chapter.

Write out your "elevator pitch" for the Three Foot Rule:

_____

_____

_____

_____

_____

Are you ashamed of your business? If so, why? And how can you change that?

_____

_____

_____

_____

_____

Do you have a mindset issue about money or greed that needs to be addressed? (I highly recommend reading *You Are a Badass at Making Money* by Jen Sincero).

_____

_____

_____

_____

_____

What additional skills do you need to feel truly confident in business? (ie. sales, process, strategy, etc.)

_____

_____

_____

_____

What type of award would matter to your client?

_____

_____

_____

_____

Pufferfish Technique:

What type of award matters to your company and staff?

_____

_____

_____

_____

_____

What award(s) can you apply for to increase your exposure?

_____

_____

_____

_____

Are there any changes that need to be made (or better documented) for the sake of an award?

_____

_____

_____

_____

6

Give Back to the Community

NUMEROUS ARTICLES HAVE BEEN WRITTEN ON THE VALUE that companies get for community involvement and philanthropy. They cite studies showing that businesses with a give back mentality have a positive financial impact on their bottom line. Most companies that have the desire to give back don't do it for this purpose, but it is a bit like Fate giving a reward for your generosity and charity. But there is another reason for giving back that you may not have considered, and that's Millennials.

Millennials are the largest generation since the Baby Boomers, and they are currently entering the workforce. While there are endless jokes about how frustrating they can be, the truth is, as employers, we need to understand how to work with them if we are going to have a successful workforce. Working for a socially responsible company is one known priority of Millennials.

Pufferfish Technique:
BE A THOUGHT LEADER

So, as we look at hiring, we need to understand what type of culture is attractive to the types of employees we want. Sometimes, this means getting creative – for us that meant creating more awareness around the worker shortage we have in our industry and finding ways to circumvent it, such as:

Video Plumber® – Allows us to work smarter by creating an opportunity for technicians with the skill, but potentially not the physical ability, to provide a quote. We see this product as an opportunity to help disabled employees, such as veterans, with plumbing and/or HVAC skills to work from a desk, rather than in the field. They have the ability to write quotes and order parts for another technician to complete the work, saving time and money.

PHCC – Participating in an association, in this case the Plumbing-Heating-Cooling Contractor Association, who lobbies for more vocational training, scholarships and education to address the looming skills gap in the trades.

Other associations will lobby for small business rights and interests, fair business practices and more. Aligning yourself with professional organizations can give teeth to the specific needs you have and affect change.

TedX – This platform allowed me, along with two other successful women in the trades who I've met along the way, to spread the word more publicly about the skills gap, encouraging women to consider the trades. TedX gave me a platform to share about this topic in a much broader way. If you haven't considered it before, I encourage you to look into the opportunities in your area.

Creating a Culture – I've mentioned before that we built into our culture the idea of corporate give back. As a company we volunteer at a local food bank, and employees are encouraged to tell us about situations that come up where we may be of service. This includes Habitat for Humanity projects and any needs from their church or other organizations they participate in.

Sustainability – This is a hot topic for young people, but is even more important to many Coloradans who want to keep the state beautiful. My husband, William Frew, formerly installed solar and is an avid rock climber. He brings this passion for the environment into our work practices. The use of technology and thoughtful management practices have allowed our company to embrace sustainability. The use of an iPad allows us to eliminate paper invoices or work orders, all billing and filing is also paperless, and GPS units on our trucks provide better gas efficiency. We also practice recycling of scrap metal, including water heaters and other plumbing and heating supplies. In addition, we have a company-wide practice of always bringing plumbing up to code and encouraging the use of the highest efficiencies put in place by the National Appliance Energy Conservation Act.

When you are thinking about community give-back, consider WHO you want as employees and what's important to them, then build a culture that provides that. Most employees will follow the leader, so if animals are important to you, they will likely be important to your employees as well. If you choose to give back to the community with animal-related charities, then prospective employees who value that will be more likely to work with you. Think about this when you choose how to give back and what types of people that will then attract as employees.

Culture includes aligning policies, procedures, KPI's... everything towards the goals you want the company to achieve and work towards. Too often ideals are expressed in a vision or mission statement, but aren't truly demonstrated in the day-to-day workings of the business. Again, this can come back to the unwillingness to change. However, to have a truly successful company, you must examine where there is misalignment and what type of culture you are creating.

In the beginning, our give back culture consisted of putting peanut butter and jelly sandwiches on every truck for the technicians to hand out to homeless people. We now laugh at the number of smashed sandwiches we would find during inventory. After all, our technicians weren't driving around looking for homeless people, they were working. We decided instead to put dog biscuits on the trucks. These were non-perishable and could be given to our clients' dogs which were a lot easier to come by. We also decided to start serving at the food bank on a quarterly basis which gave us a direct connection to those we wished to serve without the stink of rotten sandwiches in our vans.

Some other examples of the community give back that set us apart include:

- Performing repair and maintenance for an elderly woman on a fixed income
- Donating 20 hours of labor and supplies to restore the home of a family who lost their dad to a dangerous gas leak that made their home unlivable
- Fixing leaks and restoring water service to a women's victim center.

We've talked in another chapter about shameless self-promotion, and there are times when we've let media know the types of work we do for the community. However, there are other times we keep it more discreet, sharing it in specific situations, like this book, and awards applications, or even just with our team. It often has to do with the sensitivity of the service. For example, it would be unsafe to disclose the location of a women's victim center, or further disrupt a family who has experienced tremendous loss. However, consider the times and types of ways you can use the promotion of your community service so that it positions you as a Pufferfish. Which brings us to my personal favorite community give back that we offer.

The Birth of Thiftinista

While networking, speaking, or even out in public, I am often complimented on my attire. People ask me where I bought it, and most people are surprised when I tell them how little I spent by purchasing my look at a thrift store. The truth is, I am a recessionista. Before the recession, I shopped in high-end stores. Style and fashion are important to me, so I know about designers and brands. I refused to give up my favorites even when I didn't have the income to support buying them new. But because of my experience, I was able to find my favorite brands and styles easily.

Well, one day I was having a conversation with my marketing company – Crazy Good Marketing – about an idea I had to offer a bus trip to thrift stores. She liked the idea and said I should have Sunshine sponsor it, therefore highlighting the company to our demographic that was made up of 80% women. Thriftinista became a public relations stunt designed to get in front of our target market – women – and offer something of value to our community – shopping at local thrift stores.

Sunshine was able to collaborate with another marketing power partner, CampExperience™ Network, a networking and philanthropic organization we are involved with. A chartered bus was lent to us, free of charge, and women lined up to purchase bus tickets for the day-long event. The participants met at Sunshine for a light breakfast and were offered coupons for Sunshine's plumbing and heating services. They then loaded the bus and received a short talk featuring shopping tips and an opportunity to create a plan. I assisted them with shopping and getting the best deal at four thrift stores that day. The thrift stores benefited from the sales, but they also received a portion of the fares the women paid for the bus trip. A catered box lunch was served on the bus and the feedback we received after that first event was phenomenal. We have continued to offer these bus trips and have donated over $10,000 for

Goodwill, Rotary Club, and Stout Street Residential Treatment Facility in the last year (2018).

A Note About Employees

When you create a culture of community give back, it will permeate your entire company for the better. In another chapter you will hear about our benefits package which is very attractive to our employees - a way to give back to the community by creating a valuable employment culture. Community give back, along with some of our crazy benefits we offer employees aren't known to them when they are hired, but instead they experience it while working with us. Those who don't align with our values will move on, and we are okay with this.

Too often I hear business owners settle for employees who can perform a specific task, but don't fit the values of the company simply because they don't want to find a replacement. At our company, we'd rather have the right type of employee, instead of just any employee. Part of community give back is having employees who are on board with it, and also experience it themselves. You will see an increase in morale if employees are treated as well as any community service you perform.

Are you ready to dive in deeper?

Let's take some time to dive into the questions we asked earlier in the chapter.

Pufferfish Technique:

What ways can you establish yourself as a thought leader in your industry?

_____

_____

_____

_____

_____

What organizations can you support in your community?

_____

_____

_____

_____

What ways can you give back in ways that are meaningful to your target market?

_____

_____

_____

_____

What give back opportunities do your employees value?

_____

_____

_____

_____

_____

How can you use community give back as a way to attract Millennials?

_____

_____

_____

_____

How can you give back in a way that your potential clients and media will notice?

_____

_____

_____

_____

7

Create a Star Team

BECAUSE DOING GOOD WORK IS PLACED IN THE HANDS OF our employees, we treat them well. We offer what some call *crazy* benefits. Our benefits, as mentioned before, help us attract and retain quality employees. Some of our current crazy benefits include:

NO ON-CALL HOURS. To readers outside the service industry it might seem weird that we don't make our workers rotate being on call for emergencies during nights, weekends and holidays.

It is an industry standard to rotate employees in this role, which means they give up time with their families during those extra shifts. You can imagine then how not having this requirement for our employees is a huge benefit to them. We simply don't work our technicians after hours, and instead find other ways to help our clients during emergencies (such as those outlined in our 12-Points of Love). Again, this may require a shift in your perspective, and it may force you to do things differently than you've always done or how you've seen it done in your industry. Disrupt the barrier that's preventing this, and just see what happens!

UNLIMITED PERSONAL TIME OFF. Our employees can have an unlimited amount of unpaid time off. As long as it is not abused, we don't count their requested days off. We understand everyone has business to handle - from doctor appointments to school programs - so we allow it. Those who abuse this often don't stay with us long.

FLEXIBLE SCHEDULING. Once our staff have shown reliability, professionalism and the ability to work independently, they have the option of a flexible schedule within our needs. This means they may work swing shifts or four 10-hour days rather than a standard work week. Some hours can be done remotely as well, since we are a paperless company.

LEGALSHIELD. As employers, we can't advise our staff about divorce, child support, driving tickets or other legal issues. LegalShield gives employees access to legal support at discounted rates and offers some free services. This allows them to keep their mind on work and not on looming legal issues. We have found this gives everyone a lot of peace of mind since they have someone to talk to about legal issues.

In addition, because we provide it, our employees can't use it to sue us. One of the most interesting pieces of advice I've heard is that you never want an employee sitting at home watching TV during the day. This is the time when lawyers run ads, and this gives bored people the idea to call and see how much money they are entitled to. Injured, disgruntled employees with financial problems may see your company as a cash cow and will get creative at times to milk that cow. The LegalShield service covers your employees with the support they need, while also helping to protect the company from erroneous employee lawsuits. (Of course, if they are injured on the job, that is handled through Worker's Compensation - we are talking about injuries off the clock here).

FINANCIAL PEACE UNIVERSITY. Dave Ramsey is well-known in the financial community as a top speaker, author and teacher on financial wellness. While sometimes controversial, we have found his *Financial Peace University* to offer sound advice. After being asked on several occasions by different staff for payroll advances, we wanted a solution that improved morale and maintained integrity. Instead of giving advances, we pay for staff to attend *Financial Peace University*. When they build their $1000 emergency fund, as suggested in the program, we give $250 as a contribution to their savings account.

PRIZE POINTS. Reviews are huge in my world, and we wanted to incentivize our technicians to get them. If you find us online, you will see we have over 2,000 reviews. We get them because we ask every single customer to provide one, and we ask them more than once. Then, we give our technicians prizes for getting them. The biggest prize was for a trip to Mexico.

Time out for a moment here for those of you asking how we can send a technician to Mexico. We have 2,000 reviews. It costs us nothing to get these reviews beyond the cost of the prizes, yet they allow us to save the money we would have to spend on pay-per-click advertising because Google loves us! That is well worth the $3,000 price tag of a Mexican trip. Some companies spend this amount each month--we spend it once a year and make a huge positive impact on our reputation, our bottom line, and in the life of our employee.

SURPRISES. We also randomly (but strategically) offer surprises, for example, we had the Red Wing boot truck show up at a staff meeting and the guys got to pick a pair. Of course, any other gear they wanted, they purchased. We give a great breakfast spread at staff meetings. We surprise our clerical staff with tickets to galas we attend, or get a block of tickets to a Rockies Game so we can connect more as a company.

BUT WAIT, there's more. We also offer paid training, vacation pay, a health club membership, plus dental, vision, life and health insurance, all at different levels of tenure. We also pay our staff when they work at our quarterly volunteer day.

Sometimes people look at me cross-eyed wondering how we can afford benefits like this, but I see it two ways. First, it's an investment in keeping my staff happy, customer-focused and not shopping for other job opportunities. Secondly, with the current workforce crisis, how can you afford not to. In order to give our employees these benefits, we have to have profits in our business. If you see profits as bad or greedy, get over it or get out, because profits allow us the ability to reward our technicians for their skills in a way that allows them to provide for their families. Our guys are not out there buying jets, they are hard-working, just like your staff. One of our awards, one that we are very proud of, is being chosen as the one of *Denver Business Journal's* Best Places to Work in 2017. If you are struggling to find and retain staff, how beneficial could it be to your organization to be named a best place to work?

Hiring Smarter

We also work really hard to hire the best person right from the start. William created a visual test, that shows us exactly what our candidates know and don't know. When I say visual, I mean it. You have to know who your staff are, and for us, we are hiring technicians – they work with their hands with tangible products. We need to know that they know how to do these very physical things, so we test them in that way. A resume tells you what an employee's experience is, but it doesn't tell you what they can actually do.

For example, as part of our application process, we screen the technicians by having them match parts in a way that provides a solution to a problem. What if you had an employee perform a function of their job for you as part of the application and/or interview process? What if in the interview stage you had them pull a toilet, disconnect a water heater, or solder a pipe, so you could really see them work? Consider how that might look within your industry. Be sure not to just watch their technical skill, but also look at how they do it. We are watching for how they are under pressure, how they respond when something goes wrong, and what their manners are like with customers.

We also conduct a DISC assessment to discover employee's strengths and potential weaknesses. (We use Employee Development Systems - edsiusa.com). This assessment directs how we train and teach them and how we incentivize them. You don't have to use DISC, but look at what assessments you can use to help you better understand your staff. To create the best team, you should know what motivates and inspires your employees and understand how they will interact with customers. You should also discover how they work, both under supervision and independently. Lastly, you should learn about their values and understand how that aligns with your company culture.

Pufferfish Technique:

USE TECHNOLOGY TO STANDARDIZE PROCESSES

We are all human. We understand that everyone is different and will do things according to who they are. Because of this, we have put systems in place that ensure consistency and are automated whenever possible. This way the customer has the same experience, regardless of the technician who provides the service. Some things we do include:

We answer the phone the same way every time (this includes our answering service)
We send an email to the customer prior to arrival so they know who to expect (automated)
We call when we are on the way
We provide a quote before service (automated)
Clients receive a copy of their invoice via email immediately after service (automated)
Clients are asked to provide a review
Clients get a Thank You note
Some clients get a gift

You probably recognize these from our 12 Points of Love, but the concept here is to create the structure to provide consistency and whenever possible, use technology to overcome the obstacle of human error, preference, personality or habit.

Remember too, that when it comes to consistency, it starts with setting a goal, seeing where and how you are falling short, adjusting, tracking, and adjusting again. This will show you where your processes have holes and help you create long-lasting outcomes. But keep in mind, if it stops working or is no longer a priority, don't continue doing it just because you always have. Keep growing and innovating to stay fresh and in alignment with your evolving goals.

Addressing a Workforce Shortage

If you are responsible for hiring in a trade, I don't need to tell you there is a workforce shortage. For those of you who don't know this, let me take a moment to talk about this, as it's dear to my heart, and will affect all American consumers.

I'm the daughter of a carpenter, so I've always been comfortable in the blue-collar world. In fact, in my coaching practice, I unintentionally coached 17 different trades. So when I married a plumber and started our company, it wasn't long before I realized we had a huge problem. We had some great guys working for us, but when we needed more, we ran ads, and more ads, put out flyers, offered referral fees…but no one would show up.

We even offered a $1,000 sign-on bonus only to find out that a competitor had a $10,000 one. A little company like ours just couldn't compete. About a year later, we joined the Plumbing-Heating-Cooling Contractors (PHCC) Association and connected with thousands of other contractors around the country just like us who were having the same problem. They are doing great things to help solve the problem of worker shortages in our industries. On the legislative front, they are lobbying our government for funds for trade and vocational education, and on the educational side they are putting together apprenticeship programs and online training courses.

Right now in our country we have a skills gap. For the last 20 years we have pushed all of our kids to go to college and get a four-year degree, whether it was a good fit for them or not. So now we have a potential workforce with college degrees and student loan debt but no jobs. On the other hand, the trades have been overlooked and ignored. In fact, it is projected that we will have a shortage of one million construction trade workers over the next 3-5 years. (Source: National Center for Construction Education and Research, NCCER.org.)

When I was in school, I had the opportunity to go to cooking school. I went to high school in the morning and cooking school in the afternoon. Many others were given vocational opportunities such as auto and diesel mechanics, cosmetology, welding, carpentry/woodshop, electronics, agricultural studies and more. Those programs hardly exist anymore. Schools are now getting funding for STEM (Science, Technology, Engineering, Math) programs, but trades are being cut or only offered as additional programming.

What's also happening is that Baby Boomers, the largest segment of the population, are aging out of the workforce, but no one is lined up to take their place. Additionally, NCCER reports skilled construction trade worker as the hardest jobs to fill.

What does this shortage mean for Americans? It means that if you want to have work done on your house (or your car for that matter), you are going to wait. If you want to build a home, or a building, or add an addition, you are going to wait. You are also going to pay more for the service. And this creates an interesting dynamic. The law of supply and demand goes into effect – the demand for service providers will be high and the supply will be low, so it will cost more. The technicians will charge more, which means they will earn more, which may, in turn, cause more people to seek these jobs. What if you (or your children) could be ahead of the curve and get involved now? What if we encouraged learning a trade, making good money, and being proud of our craft? What if instead of getting into debt, we were able to work a trade and get paid while we are training and have money for college later when we decide to go back (to learn to be a business owner or supervisor)?

Last year, when I was working on our strategic plan, I observed that 80% of our clients are women. It made me wonder if these women would like to have a female technician. Many women are concerned about letting workers into their home, and they want someone who is detail-oriented and concerned about cleanliness. What if a female technician could overcome some of those concerns and create a new level of trust?

And here's another thing about the trades to consider – it is no longer about brawn. Today's trades require a higher level of customer service such as managing your clients and making them happy. It is about strategic thinking, critical skills and technology. In fact, since we are a completely paperless company, if you don't have technology skills, you won't work out very well. Technological innovation is changing the way business is being done. Our company has a patented and trademarked product called Video Plumber® which allows us to offer customers an estimate via video feed. We are a microwave society – we want everything fast and done now, so we created a way to make estimates faster and easier than ever.

Why do I mention this? Because I started digging in and looking at some statistics and I was shocked. If there are approximately 200,000 women in our armed forces and more than 15% of all women are in law enforcement, why are less than 3% of women in trades? There's really no better time for women to work in the trades. Here are some statistics to consider, keeping in mind that one million person shortage I mentioned and the resulting wage increases due to this shortage…

Less than 1% of HVAC (heating, ventilation and air conditioning) employees are women. Less than 2% of plumbers are. Female electricians make up about 2.2% of that trade. Carpenters have women representing only 1.6% of their workforce. Sheet metal workers are lumped in with manufacturing, so that number is a little bit higher at 2.5%. Electrical power line installers come in at 1.6% of their workforce being women. The sad truth is that our society has said that trades are a man's job. Maybe in the past, the physical requirements have kept women from doing some jobs, but what if we could start filling this one million person shortage with the right women? Do women know these jobs are available to them? Do they know there are scholarships and grants where women can earn money for apprenticing in a trade? She could get paid while earning an education. Maybe then her next step could be like my friend Linda Hudak, a plumber in Ohio, who is a Master Plumber and a small business owner.

When a woman does this, she could still go back to college later for an undergraduate degree then on to MBA, or become a project superintendent or an engineer… all those things are still on the table for her. However, she can join a trade straight out of high school and without the debt often associated with a college degree. Let's teach our sons AND daughters that working in the trades is more than okay; it's challenging and rewarding, and the opportunities are endless.

―――――

Are you ready to dive in deeper?

Let's take some time to dive into the questions we asked earlier in the chapter.

What can you put into place that would allow you to hire smarter?

_____

_____

_____

_____

_____

What is *really* important to prospective team members that you can offer as a benefit?

_____

_____

Pufferfish Technique:

_____

_____

_____

What traits are important to you to see in employees and how can you bring that out in them?

_____

_____

_____

_____

_____

What out of the box benefits can you offer employees that you may not have considered before?

_____

_____

_____

_____

_____

What technology can you implement to support a more consistent customer experience?

_____

_____

_____

_____

_____

Do you need to address a workplace shortage? What are some new ways you could overcome that?

_____

_____

_____

_____

_____

8

Pulling it All Together

WHEN YOU TAKE A LOOK AT WHAT MAKES A PUFFERFISH and begin to intentionally implement the strategies, one step at a time, you will see results. Don't worry about doing everything right away, but rather deciding what you can do now and building towards more. As a recap, here are some of the techniques we shared:

NEVER RELY on what's always been done to justify anything

You can not be a thought leader if you are unwilling or unable to change. Be innovative by always looking to improve.

TRACK EVERYTHING and adjust based on the results

You can't know what to change if you don't know where you've been. You don't know how to improve or what to adjust if you don't track.

. . .

DOCUMENT what you are doing and share it like crazy

You are likely already doing amazing things. Be sure to make it official and start promoting the good you do.

MAXIMIZE REVIEWS

Follow up with clients and ask specifically for feedback in the form of reviews. Good reviews should be shared everywhere and poor reviews should be handled in a way to improve customer service.

APPLY FOR AWARDS

Find awards that are important to you, your employees and your customers and then put in the sweat to apply for and win them.

BE a thought leader

Be innovative – always looking for new ways to solve old problems. Find or create a platform for being an expert in your field.

USE TECHNOLOGY TO standardize processes

Utilize all the technology available to create streamlined, automatic, and easy processes so you can scale up and provide consistency.

IN ADDITION, you should build the following into your Pufferfish company culture:

- Doing good work – define it and follow it.
- Being a networking rock star – show up and sparkle.
- Delivering outstanding customer service – be known for your service in your industry.
- Shamelessly self-promoting – shout from the rooftops about who you are and what you are doing in the world, because what you are doing matters.
- Giving back to the community – make giving back part of what makes you attractive to the people you serve.
- Creating the best team – build a team around you that supports you, your business, and your community in whole.

By following these guidelines, you can create a Puffer-fish Effect and experience success as a business owner. Nothing is perfect. Your plan helps lays a foundation for what you want to achieve, but it is never a straight line. There will be days when you will make tremendous strides and others when you want to give up. Entrepreneurship is not for the faint of heart.

You can be a Pufferfish. In fact, you owe it to your business, your employees and your customers to be. Here's to your success!

About the Author

As the woman behind the success of Sunshine Plumbing Heating Air in Denver, Colorado, Susan Frew shares valuable knowledge and insight to companies and contractors in the home service industry.

If you're on a search for an inspiring and experienced thought leader in the home service industry, look no further than Susan Frew. A successful businesswoman with over 20 years of experience, Susan offers valuable insights and personal, engaging stories that are memorable, motivational, and informational. Susan was a certified and trained business coach, driving more than 17 different trades to great triumph including her own company, Sunshine Plumbing Heating Air, the PHC News "Contractor of the Year".

If you are tired of Leadership Speakers who have never lead, or Motivational Speakers who have never had a team of employees, look no further than Susan Frew.

As your keynote speaker, Susan can deliver a dynamic speech that is focused on the theme of your event. She is well-versed in a vast array of subject matters regarding the home service industry from increasing company revenues to keeping the millennial workforce happy, empowering women in the trade, and more.

Whether keynotes, breakout sessions, or bootcamps, Susan is ready to reveal the secrets to creating a profitable business. Learn more and contact her for availability at: https://www.susanrobertsfrew.com/contact/